SIX LITTLE CHICKADEES

Nine little kinglets! Cordelia Stanwood made studies of birds as fierce as hawks and birds whose chicks were no larger than bumblebees.

Ada Graham

SIX LITTLE CHICKADEES

A Scientist and her Work with Birds

FOUR WINDS PRESS   NEW YORK

LIBRARY OF CONGRESS
CATALOGING IN PUBLICATION DATA

Graham, Ada.
  Six little chickadees.

  Summary: Presents some of the career work done by Cordelia Stanwood, who began her study of birds when orni-
thology was a very young science.
  1. Stanwood, Cordelia, 1865–1958—Juvenile literature.
2. Ornithologists—United States—Biography—Juvenile literature. [1. Stanwood, Cordelia, 1865–1958. 2. Ornithologists]
I. Title.
QL31.S67G7   598.092′4 [B] [92]   82-5055
ISBN 0-590-07508-X   AACR2

PUBLISHED BY FOUR WINDS PRESS

A DIVISION OF SCHOLASTIC INC., NEW YORK, N.Y.

PRINTED IN THE UNITED STATES OF AMERICA

LIBRARY OF CONGRESS CATALOG CARD NUMBER: 82-5055

1 2 3 4 5 86 85 84 83 82

Contents

SIX LITTLE CHICKADEES

Cordie walked back to her home, which she called Birdsacre.

PART I

BEPPO THE CROW

CHAPTER I

A *discovery*

Cordie Stanwood was walking home from town. It was a bright, spring morning in Maine nearly eighty years ago.

She looked up and saw a crow fly over the road. The crow was carrying something in its beak.

Cordie saw a second crow. It followed close behind the first one. It also carried something in its beak.

She watched both crows land in a young pine tree on the edge of the woods.

They must be returning to a nest, she thought.

She walked slowly toward the woods. Then she carefully ran her

At the top of the pine tree was the crows' nest.

eyes up each tall evergreen. She saw a dark mass of twigs near the top of a pine. It must be the nest of the crows.

She watched the crow family come and go. They were caring for their young in the nest.

Could I keep a crow-baby at home? she wondered.

Cordie walked quickly back to her home, which she had named Birdsacre. She made up her mind to adopt one of the chicks in that nest high in the tree.

I will learn how crows behave, she told herself.

2

Raymond was an excellent climber.

The next morning Cordie set out for the woods. She had thought all night about the chicks in the nest.

Raymond, a boy who lived across the road, was helping her carry a tall wooden ladder.

"It isn't very far from here, Raymond," she said. They moved through the brush and the scrubby trees to the deep woods. They could see the big nest built of sticks.

"Over there!" she pointed excitedly. At the top of the pine tree was the crows' nest.

The parent crows began to fly in circles, calling loudly and strongly. They wanted to frighten away the woman and the boy who were carrying the ladder. Crows had many enemies. Most people thought they were pests because they ate corn and grain from planted fields. They also ate eggs from the nests of other birds.

3

Crows should be killed, people said, and they often were.

Cordie and her helper, Raymond, stood at the bottom of the tree. They put the ladder in place. They tested it several times to make sure it was secure.

Cordie thought of the hours she had spent in these woods since she had returned to Maine.

For many years she had been a teacher in Massachusetts. But she became ill and had to come home to Maine. Now she was trying to grow strong and well again.

For many years Cordie had been a teacher.

4

Her heart pounded as Raymond mounted the tall ladder. But she did not need to be afraid. Raymond was an excellent climber.

He reached the nest and carefully lifted out one of the dark gray birds. The tiny helpless chick had not yet grown any feathers. Raymond came down the ladder, carefully holding the chick.

Cordie took the chick from the boy. It struggled weakly in her hand.

I can care for him at home in a box of fresh hay, she thought. I will call him Beppo.

CHAPTER 2

A new home

Cordie fed Beppo every hour. She gave him hard-boiled eggs, mashed potatoes, oatmeal, and milk. She even gave him some of her dog Brownie's biscuits that had been soaked in water.

That evening she fed him a generous dose of earthworms.

She noticed that the tips of his wing feathers were beginning to show through their coverings. His feet and legs were already heavy and strong.

The bird, she guessed, was about ten days old.

At night Cordie covered his box with a warm woolen coat. He needed little care.

He ate, slept, and grew.

When he was nearly three weeks old, Beppo stood for the first time. Cordie was very excited.

She wrote about him in her notebook: "Beppo now began hopping, climbing and perching."

"Beppo now began hopping, climbing and perching," Cordie wrote.

Every day his wings became a little stronger. He hopped a little higher until he began to fly.

Soon Beppo could fly as high as the topmost branch of the pine tree in the yard.

Cordie would stand below the bird for hours, talking to him, before he would come down.

No effort was too great for her to make Beppo happy.

6

CHAPTER 3
Friends

By the time Beppo was three weeks old he knew that the tall figure was his mistress. He would come to her whenever she appeared.

He liked to be near Cordie. She felt that Beppo was jealous when others shared her attention.

Crows are very intelligent birds. They are curious and active. Beppo began to pick up anything that was bright and shiny.

He began to fly to Cordie's lap and to perch on her shoulder.

Beppo followed her into the woods. They looked very funny together—the tall woman in a long skirt, followed by the little crow with his self-important walk.

He was always alert on their walks. If he heard the creak of a tree or the call of another crow, he would stop and listen.

When Beppo was five weeks old, he took his first bath at a spring in the woods. When he finished his bath he climbed to Cordie's shoulder. Then he mounted her head. He shook off the drops of water. He straightened his feathers. Cordie laughed at her crow-baby.

He caught and ate frogs, caterpillars, moths, dragonflies, grasshoppers, crickets, salamanders, moles, and mice.

Once the young crow caught his prey, it never escaped him.

Beppo had become independent.

When a person adopts a bird at a very early age, that person becomes its parent. Beppo looked on Cordie as his parent.

On May 15 the crow had steak for his breakfast. In the afternoon, Beppo and Cordie took a walk in the woods.

When they returned to the barn, Beppo "talked" and laughed.

"I could hear him from the house through the closed windows," his mistress wrote. Later she went to the woods to watch the nest of another family of birds.

"At night before the barn was closed I looked to see if Beppo had gone to roost," she wrote. "He could not be found. I called him. I went to the other houses he visited. No one had seen him."

Two days of watching and wondering dragged on.

The next morning a neighbor found jolly little Beppo in her barn. He was lying in the hay, dead. He had been shot.

CHAPTER 5
Cordie makes a plan

Cordie could not believe it at first. How could anyone kill the friendly bird, Beppo?

When she realized it was true, she ran to her room. She slammed the door behind her. She stayed there for several days.

Everyone knew how attached she had grown to Beppo. Her family feared that she would make herself ill again. She ate almost nothing. She talked to no one. The killing of her little friend made no sense to her and she was angry about it.

She never learned who had killed Beppo.

By the time Cordie felt strong enough to come out of the room and face the world again, she knew what she wanted to do.

She made up her mind to tell the world about birds.

If we knew what happened in the lives of birds, she thought, we would understand how important they are in our own lives.

"I will go on trying to discover how birds live," she wrote in her notebook. "I will try to find a way to share my experience with other people."

She made up her mind to tell the world about birds. This tiny bird is a redstart.

11

PART II

THE CHICKADEE FAMILY

CHAPTER 6

A *new science*

The study of birds was a new science. There were not many men who knew much about how birds behaved around their nests. There were almost no women who knew about those things.

Many scientists who studied birds worked only in museums. They studied the feathers and skeletons of birds.

A new group of scientists was interested in watching how birds lived. They spent their time watching live birds around their nests. It was possible to see birds well when they came together at the nest.

Cordie Stanwood was doing this work at Birdsacre. From early in the morning until late at night, she spent her time in the woods. She carefully watched the small birds in spring and summer.

12

Cordie watched the chicks and their parents from a hiding place called a brush blind.

If she followed them, they might lead her to the secret places they had chosen to start their nests. One summer morning she followed two small, greenish birds into the woods.

The birds tried out many places. They landed first on one branch, then on another. The female fitted her body to a space in a forked branch. The bird was satisfied at last.

Cordie watched the birds carry each piece of building material to the site they had chosen for a nest.

She watched them bring bark from dead trees, curls of birch bark, bits of the homes of paper wasps, down from pussy willows, parts of soft, green lichen plants, moss, and the silk from spiders' webs and caterpillars' cocoons. Every item that came to the nest in the beaks of the tiny birds was recorded in Cordie's notebook.

She thought of these birds as "love-birds" when she watched the little ceremony that took place as materials were delivered to the nest. The birds stood close to each other and sang sweet notes. They moved their beaks up and down as though bowing to one another.

Finally one bird sat in the nest, pressing the materials into shape, making them stronger for the family it would hold.

When the birds had lined the nest with the fine shredded fibers of last year's goldenrod stems, it was ready for the mother bird and her eggs.

"The birds had spent six days building their nest," Cordie wrote.

Cordie watched the mother bird turn her four eggs with her beak. The shells were beginning to weaken. Near the eighth day, a crack began to appear at the end of one of the eggs. Finally the egg split open. The chick was free.

The female fitted her body to a space in a forked branch.

When Cordie came to the nest on the morning of July 1, she found four young birds. The nest was just large enough to hold the hungry, sleepy chicks.

When Cordie came to the nest, she found four chicks.

16

A canvas blind.

Cordie watched every movement of the chicks and their parents from a hiding place she had made of evergreen boughs. This hiding place was called a blind.

She could see the chicks' huge heads and stomachs. Their legs were short and weak, but their mouths were large and often open! The parts of their stomachs showed through their featherless skin. Even their eyeballs showed through the closed lids of their eyes.

Cordie was so close to the nest that she could hear the parent birds catching flies and mosquitoes.

She carefully kept track of the number of times the parent birds brought food to the nest. She counted sixteen trips made by the father to the nest with food, and fourteen trips made by the mother, in the four hours that she watched. The birds were fed during that time every eight minutes by one of the parents, she figured.

Cordie observed birds leaving their nests in every part of Birds-acre. Here are four young flycatchers.

Cordie listed every beetle, caterpillar, moth, grub, or fly that was brought to the nest.

She watched the tiny birds become active—yawning, stretching, standing up, and scratching their heads with their toes.

The chicks became covered with feathers. When Cordie arrived at the nest on the ninth day, she heard the chatter of the birds in the tree tops. The little birds had left the nest.

18

Cordie observed nests and their families in every part of Birdsacre. She found them hanging from branches, on the ground, in low shrubs, and even in the cavities of trees.

Soon she knew as much about the nesting life of birds in the woods as any other scientist in the country. Alone, teaching herself, she had made many discoveries in this new science.

 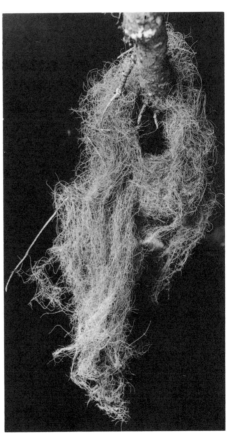

Nests: Some birds used bark from dead trees.

Other birds used the soft green plant, lichen, to make a hanging nest.

19

CHAPTER 7

The camera

Cordie wanted to share the results of her studies with other people. She wanted to see them published in books and magazines.

At the same time, she still had many questions about birds. She could not find the answers to them in the books she read.

So she wrote to a famous scientist at the American Museum of Natural History. His name was Frank M. Chapman. He was able to give Cordie some help.

He answered questions about birds. He told her that it might be difficult at that time for a woman to have her scientific work published.

But other magazines looked for stories about birds, especially if there were good photographs to illustrate them.

Her Aunt Cordelia, for whom she had been named, had died recently. She had left Cordie some money. Cordie sent the money to Dr. Chapman and asked him to order a good camera for her.

The Kodak camera finally arrived. It was large and bulky, as all cameras were many years ago.

When Cordie opened the stout leather case, the new Kodak looked just like a box. But there was a book of instructions with the camera.

Cordie opened the box and drew out the lens. She stood the camera on a stand and looked through it.

I know I will be able to take good pictures in the woods, she told herself. I will start tomorrow.

I know I will be able to take good pictures in the woods, she told herself.

21

CHAPTER 8

A nest in the stump

Cordie hung a piece of cotton on the end of a branch in the yard. Then she walked back into the house.

She waited.

Chickadee-dee-dee!

Chickadee-dee-dee!

Yes, it was the call of the bird she had been waiting for, the black-capped chickadee. She went to the kitchen window.

Perched in the bush outside the window were two little birds.

Their backs were gray. They had tiny black caps and black chins. *Chickadee-dee-dee!* The two birds called back and forth to each other. *Chickadee-dee-dee!* They repeated their name with each call.

She watched carefully as a chickadee pulled at bits of the cotton. The little bird held the cotton down with her feet. Then she tore off pieces with her bill. Her bill was filled with the fluffy cotton.

The two birds called and flew away toward an old stone wall in the field.

Cordie rushed to the door, opened it, and followed the birds into the woods.

In a few moments she reached the stone wall where she discovered the broken stump of an old tree. When she looked closely, she found a hole in the stump. The birds had dug out the hole. They had lined it with moss, fern down, and fine hair.

It was the call of the bird she had been waiting for, the black-capped chickadee.

23

In the bottom of the hole lay a piece of cotton. Cordie knew that she had come to the right spot.

She had hung this piece of cotton on a bush, hoping some birds would take it and lead her to their nest.

Cordie felt that she was ready to photograph the nesting life of a family of birds.

She could not have guessed that the nest of this chickadee family would someday become famous.

CHAPTER 9
The big storm

Cordie visited the chickadees' nest in the stump whenever she could. She did not want to disturb the birds. She saw that one of the birds was sitting on its eggs. One day, as she returned from the nest, it began to rain.

It rained and rained then, for days at a time.

Cordie worried. Would the nest be flooded? Would the eggs get cold? Would the mother and father birds leave the nest? From her long experience she knew so many things could go wrong.

She would wake at night and think of the tiny bird family. She would hear the wind blow. She would listen to the rain fall.

But she need not have worried.

When she visited the nest again, she heard the chickadee call-note: *Phee-bee!*

The father arrived and perched on the edge of the nest. He carried a beak full of caterpillars. He gave them to his mate while she was sitting on the nest.

After she finished the meal, she flew away. She called to her mate and he joined her.

Cordie was excited. She came out of her hiding place and looked into the nest in the stump of the tree.

"To my great joy I saw four limp, pale orange chicks," she wrote later. "There were two eggs ready to hatch."

She walked through the wet woods. Her mind was full of plans. She could photograph this family.

Young chickadees remain in the nest about two weeks, she knew. They would be large enough for a picture in about two weeks.

Six little chickadees! she said to herself. The parents have won.

CHAPTER 10
Famous chickadees

Raymond, the boy from across the road, arrived early in the morning. He carried the heavy camera equipment into the woods.

Cordie and Raymond placed the camera very near the nest. The sun shone on the stump for only a few minutes.

Through the camera she watched the mother and father birds coming to the nest. They were bringing food to the six hungry birds. The tiny, pale orange chicks had become black and white like their parents.

25

Raymond had made a perch for the chicks. It was a branch tied to the trunk. It was open to the morning sun.

He began to place the chicks on the perch.

He started with one bird and slowly and patiently added each chick to the perch, one at a time.

All six chicks were grasping the perch with their tiny feet. Cordie was ready to snap their picture when. . . .

Chickadee-dee-dee! Off to the side, the father and mother had arrived with juicy caterpillars and large crane flies in their beaks. They were sounding the food call-note to their chicks.

Off to the side, the father had arrived with a crane fly in its beak.

The chickadees fluttered off the perch onto the ground.

What confusion followed!

Wings flapped, necks twisted, and the tiny chickadees fluttered off their perch onto the grass.

Nothing remained in focus in the camera but the branch.

Raymond returned the chicks after their meal again and again. Cordie could not count how many times.

At last pictures were taken that had each and every one of the six little chickadees clearly in focus.

"By the time we finished the last picture, most of the babes were very sleepy," Cordie wrote. "Upon being put back into their nest they snuggled down to sleep. I know that by tomorrow the whole family will be on the wing."

A national magazine was eager to take her story and her pictures.

"Your article is wonderful," the editor wrote. "We will be able to use seven of your pictures. A check will be mailed for more than our usual rate."

Everyone who saw the chickadees in the magazine, *The House Beautiful*, loved them. They had become famous all over the country.

The six little chickadees had become famous all over the country.

PART III
THE WILDEST BIRDS

CHAPTER 11
A *disappointment*

One day a letter arrived at Birdsacre.

"Our state needs a photographer to take pictures of our birds," a scientist wrote to Cordie Stanwood. "Will you take this job?"

Cordie was pleased and excited. She would be paid for doing the thing she loved most in all the world!

She wrote to the scientist and told him she would take the job.

She had already made many pictures since her adventure with the chickadees. She had sold her pictures to magazines and newspapers.

Many scientists knew about her stories and her photographs. They knew that what she told them was true.

But the scientist who had offered her a job had not asked the head of his office about Cordie. He had written too quickly.

The head of the office pointed out that Miss Stanwood was a woman.

Who would carry her equipment into the woods? Who would go with her to dangerous places? Her pictures were excellent, it was true. But he did not believe that she could do the work.

When the scientist wrote to tell Cordie that she could not have the job, she was terribly disappointed.

For several days she could not carry on her work in the woods. It took her a long time to forget that she had lost this job. She thought that it should have been hers.

This time Cordie's disappointment did not make her ill. She knew that many people admired her work. She went on studying the birds.

But she never again thought of leaving Maine. And she did not leave Birdsacre itself very often.

CHAPTER 12
Two hawks

Cordie was watching a pair of unusual birds. Broad-winged hawks were flying above the woods. They were calling back and forth to one another.

She knew from her experience that these birds were getting ready to raise a family.

That morning she set out with a folding campstool.

She spent the day in the swampy woods, listening. When she grew tired of one spot, she would take her folding stool and move to another.

31

She saw what looked like the beginning of a nest. It was about fifteen feet from the ground.

She watched and listened carefully.

As she was about to leave the woods, she saw what looked like the beginning of a nest. It was about fifteen feet from the ground.

Each time she visited the swamp she found one of the brown hawks near the tree.

She hoped they had chosen this tree in which to raise a family.

A week later she surprised one of the hawks in the nest. This nest did not look like the tight, finely woven homes of the small birds she studied. It looked more like a jumble of sticks piled onto branches in the tree.

Hawks are wild, high-flying birds. They are fierce and they are secretive. It is not easy to come close to the nest of a hawk.

Cordie loved hawks, but at that time most people hated them.

Hawks were shot, trapped, and stoned. They were killed by farmers and boys in the woods.

They were killed by lovers of other birds because hawks sometimes attacked small birds and their young.

32

Not even many bird students thought hawks were beautiful or useful.

Hawks were not protected by laws, as they are now.

Hardly anybody loved hawks, that is, except Cordie Stanwood.

She loved them for their sense of freedom and power. She loved to see them soaring high above her in the sky.

C H A P T E R   13

A climb to the nest

One morning Cordie walked to the nest. Raymond was with her. She and the boy were carrying a ladder.

As the woman and the boy came to the tree, the hawk flew up from the nest. It perched on an old stump and looked down fiercely at the visitors.

Its high, loud calls seemed to threaten Cordie and the boy.

Carefully watching the hawk, she and Raymond placed the ladder against the tree.

Cordie slowly mounted the ladder. The ladder and the cries of the hawk alarmed her. She began to feel dizzy.

The ground grew farther and farther away. She held the ladder tightly.

At last she reached the top of the ladder. She was fifteen feet above the ground. She looked down into the nest.

In the center of the circle of dead sticks lay two eggs. They were a little larger than chicken eggs. The deep cream color of the shells was streaked with many other beautiful colors.

Small, downy feathers clung to the eggs. They had worn off the breasts of the parents while they were sitting on the eggs.

Lying in the nest were two long feathers. Cordie carefully picked them up. She ran them across her hand.

She would keep them. They would remind her of the stolen moment at the hawks' nest that day.

She climbed down the ladder. The hawk called its loud, sharp cry.

As she and Raymond left the woods, the hawk followed them. It called again and again until they reached the house.

That night she took the brown hawk feathers from her pocket. She ran her fingers over them. They were soft and smooth. They were very shiny.

As she closed her eyes, she held the feathers in her hand. In her mind she saw the wild bird fly over her head. She could still hear its harsh, wild cry.

CHAPTER 14
The hunter

It was a hot afternoon in July. Cordie was walking in the woods.

The hawks' nest was only a half mile away. It now held two chicks.

Cordie crept under some evergreen trees. She wanted to rest for a moment.

She heard a faint stir. She looked down at the plants at her feet.

There was a whole family of mice. They were moving back and forth through their little runways, among the twigs.

How I wish my little hawks could have this family of mice for supper, she thought.

Suddenly there was a flash before her eyes.

The father hawk had seen these tiny forms with his sharp eyes. Perhaps he had also heard their faint voices with his keen ears.

In an instant he swept down across the path. The hawk spied Cordie just in time to avoid hitting her.

She breathed rapidly.

Cordie had just seen what few people see—a wild hunter at work.

The hawks needed to find mice, moles, snakes, and other prey to feed themselves and their young.

Cordie admired the fierce nature of these hunting birds. She thought of the down-covered chicks in the nest. They were so weak now that they could hardly hold up their heads.

Would these little birds grow to be swift, sure hunters like their parents? It was hard to believe.

Cordie decided to visit the nest every week and take pictures of the chicks. She would make a photo album of their growing up.

Would this little bird grow to be a swift, sure hunter like its parents?

35

She made the first of her weekly visits when the chicks were twelve days old. The parent birds were away hunting. She decided to name the chicks Sister and Brother.

When Cordie climbed to the nest, both birds sat up. They opened their beaks and struck at her with their feet. Even now they were fierce birds, ready to fight.

Cordie put Sister in a basket and took her down the ladder. She carried her to a tree stump in the bright sunlight. It was a good place to take a picture.

She made the first of her weekly visits when the chicks were twelve days old.

36

Each week Cordie took a picture of Brother and Sister.

The pictures showed how the feathers on the wings began to grow.

37

Their legs grew strong, too.

Cordie and Raymond kept to their plan. Every week they took pictures of Brother and Sister.

The pictures showed how the feathers on their wings and tails began to grow.

The baby hawks flapped their newly feathered wings. Cordie could see how one day they would use these strong muscles. They would soon soar high above her, riding on the air.

Their legs grew strong, too. On Cordie's fourth visit to the hawks' nest, Sister raised her claws to strike her. Her talons grazed Cordie's hand. They were so sharp they drew blood.

The bird pushed with such force that she threw herself backward out of the nest.

But the young hawk grasped a branch with the powerful talons of one foot. She dangled there, upside down.

During these five weeks Cordie took over a hundred pictures of the young hawks.

PART IV
THE PET THRUSH

CHAPTER 17
The bird in the box

Raymond knocked at the door. He was holding a shoe box. His younger sister, Laurie, was standing at his side.

"Laurie found this stray, Miss Stanwood," he said when she opened the door. "It was all alone—an orphan bird."

Cordie looked down at the brownish bird in the bottom of the box. She could see its bright eyes staring up at her.

She knew at once it was a thrush. A thrush is a bird of the deep woods. It is much like a robin.

"It's a baby thrush," she said. "Where did Laurie find the bird?"

"Over near the stone wall," Laurie said. "Across the field, near those trees." And she pointed in the direction of the woods.

"Sometimes the parent birds do leave the nest," she said.

"Perhaps we should see if the mother bird has returned," Cordie said.

The three of them walked across the field toward the woods.

"Sometimes the parent birds do leave the nest," Cordie said. "Sometimes a small bird is forced to be on its own much too early."

The nest was deserted. Cordie listened carefully. She did not hear the mother or father bird nearby.

She looked down at the box. The tiny young bird was trembling.

"All right, children," she said. "I will adopt the bird. But you must help me."

Cordie knew that it was very hard to raise a young bird. It would need a lot of care.

"I will need many insects, worms, and ant eggs to feed this young bird," she told the children. "You must help me find them."

As the three friends walked back across the field, they found some wild strawberries.

Cordie took the bird from the box. She held it gently in her hand. First the bird pulled away. Then it closed its eyes. It ate a strawberry and then became quiet in her hand.

CHAPTER 18

Pet

When Cordie reached the house, she placed the bird on a window sill. The children went to find food for the new pet.

Cordie cupped her hand around the bird. She moved an earthworm in a circle in front of its beak.

It was no use. "Pet" would not eat.

Cordie grew troubled.

She found a pair of scissors and began to cut the earthworm into bits. When the thrush heard the click of the scissors, it flew to the floor.

It opened its beak for food. It ate two earthworms that Raymond and his sister Laurie had brought. Cordie cut them up and fed them to the thrush, piece by piece, on the end of the scissors.

Then Pet, which was Cordie's name for the bird, perched on her knee.

Their friendship had begun.

CHAPTER 19
Learning to be wild

Cordie knew now that a wild bird is only happy if it is in the woods. If she did not help the tiny thrush to return to the woods, it would not learn to care for itself in time to fly south in the fall. She knew she must not grow too close to this bird.

This would not be easy to do. On the third day the thrush perched on Cordie's head. Then it snuggled against her throat.

One day, as Cordie sat at her desk writing in her diary, Pet flew from the window sill and landed on the book. The bird began to peck at her pen.

45

"It looks as though Pet wants to stop me from writing," she said, laughing.

On the fifth day it sang a baby thrush song. Cordie watched the bird pick up ant eggs from the floor and feed itself.

Pet ate larger and larger numbers of ant eggs. Raymond, Laurie, and all the other children were kept busy finding food for Pet.

Soon, the thrush was old enough to go with Cordie on walks to the woods. It ate grass, picked up earthworms, and bathed in the brook. The bird was beginning to know the outdoors again.

At the end of twelve days, Cordie knew that Pet must return to the woods soon.

The next morning she took Pet to a spot in the woods, with a brook nearby. She left it there.

She returned to this spot to feed her friend every three hours. She did not give the bird much food. She wanted Pet to learn to find food alone.

She watched the bird fly a foot into the air after mosquitoes.

At night she placed the bird on a high branch, safe from enemies.

When she returned in the morning, she always found Pet in the same spot.

She felt the bird had learned its lessons well. Pet knew where to drink and take a bath; it knew where to find mosquitoes, moths, spiders, ant eggs, grasshoppers, and earthworms. Pet knew where to hide from enemies.

She saw Pet for the last time. It was early one evening.

She called, "Pet, Pet, Pet."

The air was full of the songs of thrushes, the most beautiful sound in all the woods.

Pet answered with the call-note, *"Chunk, chunk, chunk."*

"The warm night, the moonlight, and the music of the birds were like magic," she wrote later.

For several days after this she called Pet. It never answered.

The little thrush again became a wild bird.

The little thrush again became a wild bird.

CHAPTER 20
Look! Look at the birds

Cordie Stanwood was special.

She saw something that other people in her time did not see. She saw a world filled with birds, a world filled with birds doing things that were a mystery to most other people.

Cordie found the answers to some of these mysteries. She put together the stories about these birds' lives.

She carefully watched the birds until she understood something about their lives. She found that each kind of bird lived a different life and told a different story.

"Look! Look at the birds," Cordie told us in her pictures. "They will show us things we never expected to know.

A hummingbird is the smallest of birds.

"Listen! Listen to the birds," Cordie told us in her stories. "Their songs will tell us things we never expected to understand.

"Look at the birds," Cordie said, "and they will always tell us something about themselves. They may even tell us something about ourselves."

The flicker is a large woodpecker.

49

A great horned owl sits on a stump at Birdsacre.

Birdsacre today

Cordelia Stanwood's home in Ellsworth, Maine, is now a museum.

Her notebooks, her pictures and stories, and the books she used may be seen by visitors. The typewriter she wrote her stories on is there. So is the campstool she sat on while she watched the birds.

Beppo the crow, the two hawks Brother and Sister, Pet the thrush, and the six little chickadees all lived near Birdsacre. Today people bring many birds that are sick or hurt to Birdsacre.

Birds are now carefully protected by laws. It is against the law to keep wild birds—and even to care for them—at home. Cordie's friends at Birdsacre carry on her work and care for birds.

Today, if you visit Cordie's home, you will find that her woods are still filled with birds. You can walk on the paths. Close your eyes, and you will hear the same bird songs that she heard more than seventy years ago.

The chipping sparrow makes a "chipping" sound.

Important dates in the life of Cordelia Stanwood

1865		Born, August 1, Ellsworth, Maine.
1879	Age 14	Went to Providence, Rhode Island, to live with her Aunt Cordelia and attend school.
1887	Age 22	First teaching assignment.
1904	Age 39	Became ill and returned to Ellsworth.
1905	Age 40	Began intensive studies of birds.
1909–40	Age 44–75	Wrote and published articles.
1916–26	Age 51–61	Made and printed over five hundred photos of birds.
1958	Age 93	Died in Ellsworth.

The red-eyed vireo is a bird of the forest.

54

About this book

This is a true story. It describes a woman who worked very hard to learn about birds and to tell other people about them. She took many notes. She kept diaries. She also made photographs and wrote articles.

When she grew very old she gave her pictures and her books to her friends. They formed a club to study birds. They cared for the work she left behind.

And so in this way these books and pictures have been handed down to us today. They give us a story from real life.